THE RIPARIAN RIGHTS

OF

Virginia Proprietors on the Potomac River.

WASHINGTON, *July* 12, 1859.

To HALL NEILSON, Esq.,

President of the Great Falls Manufacturing Company:

SIR: From papers submitted to us, it appears that "The Great Falls Manufacturing Company" are proprietors of a tract of land on the Virginia shore of the Potomac river, at or about the Great Falls of said river, called the "Toulson tract," and that upon this tract there are many mill sites which may be made available if the owners have a right to divert the water from the river for their use.

The riparian rights of the owners of Virginia lands on the Potomac river appear to have been for the first time judicially questioned by Judge Brewer, in pronouncing the opinion of the Circuit Court for the county of Montgomery, in the State of Maryland, on a motion to set aside a certain inquisition assessing damages for the condemnation of a portion of Conn's island, lying in Montgomery county, opposite the "Toulson tract." In that opinion the Judge declares: "I think it clear that Maryland included within its chartered limits not only the bed of the Potomac river to low water mark on the further side, but to the bank beyond, excluding the possession of any riparian rights of the State of Virginia." He also says:

"This Toulson tract has no riparian rights on the river Potomac." (Judge Brewer's opinion; Senate Ex. Doc. No. 42, 35th Cong. 2d session.)

It is in view probably of the doubt thus raised, that the question has been submitted for our opinion, "Whether the owners of the 'Toulson tract' have riparian rights in the Potomac river?" In proceeding to discuss this question, we do not deem it necessary to attempt a formal refutation of an opinion which, although entitled to great respect as proceeding from a learned and upright lawyer, possesses no judicial authority upon questions affecting the rights of Virginia proprietors, or relating to compacts between two sovereign States, and shall proceed to present our views affirmatively in relation to the question submitted, as one disembarrassed by any adjudications of the courts of Maryland.

We are of opinion that the owners of the "Toulson tract" possess riparian rights in the Potomac river, for the following reasons:

I. The rights of Maryland under the charter of 1632 to Lord Baltimore, are subject to the riparian rights previously existing by the laws of nature, by the laws of nations, and the common law, incident to the lands on the Virginia shore.

In considering this point, we shall assume that the rights conferred by the charter of Maryland to Lord Baltimore, notwithstanding the adverse claims of Virginia, were fully secured to him according to its extent and legal scope. In determining the extent of this ancient charter, we must be governed by the principle applied by the Supreme Court of the United States to the construction of the ancient charters of Massachusetts and Rhode Island. "In looking at transactions so remote," say the Court, "we must, as far as practicable, view things as they were seen and understood at the time that they transpired. There is no other test of truth and justice which applies to the variable condition of human concerns." (IV Howard's Reports, page 629.)

This principle also compels us to consider the condition of the territory which was the subject of the early Royal charters, and the causes which induced the granting of the charter of Maryland.

According to historical records, the limits of Virginia by its second charter—that of 1609, whose validity has always been maintained by the State of Virginia—extended two hundred miles North of Old Point Comfort, and therefore included all the soil which subsequently formed the State of Maryland. The colony was thus mistress of all the waters of the Chesapeake, and of the soil on both sides of the Potomac. The Episcopal Church was coeval in Virginia with the establishment of the colony. From the earliest period the most bitter prejudices existed against the professors of the Roman Catholic religion. Papists were classed by the early colonists with "players, as the scum and dregs of the earth;" (Bancroft's Hist. 1st vol. p. 142) and the careful exclusion of Roman Catholics was originally avowed as a special object in the planting of the colony. Sir George Calvert, a convert to the Roman Catholic Church, who had become early interested in the colonial establishments in America, sought an asylum in the New World for the followers of his church, from the intolerance which persecuted them at home. He looked to Virginia, then extolled for its climate and fertility. When he visited this colony in person, which he did in 1629, the zeal of the Assembly ordered the oaths of allegiance and supremacy to be tendered to him. It was in vain that he proposed a form which he was willing to subscribe; the Government firmly insisted upon that which had been chosen by the English statutes, and which was purposely framed in such language as no Catholic could adopt. Convinced that he could not hope to establish a colony within the jurisdiction of Virginia, he sought to obtain a charter which should sever a province from the colony to which so vast a territory had been assigned, and therefore penned the charter of Maryland, which was, in 1632, issued for the benefit of his son.

It is evident, from the circumstances which induced the

application for the charter, that its intent in fixing its southern boundary—namely, carrying it to the further bank of the river —was not so much to extend territorial rights, as to fix a clear and well determined natural boundary. Bancroft, the historian, speaking of Sir Charles Calvert and his charter, says: "As a Catholic, he needed to be free from the jurisdiction of his neighbor; Maryland was *carefully separated* from Virginia." (Bancroft's History, Vol. 1. p. 243.) The purpose of the charter was to relieve the new province from the religious intolerance which prevailed in Virginia. A well defined boundary was necessary to separate naturally conflicting jurisdictions. This manifest purpose would have been defeated, if the legal effect of the charter had been, as has been lately contended, to give to Maryland territorial rights and jurisdiction over the southern shores of the Potomac to high water mark, which would give to Maryland a strip of land varying in width, separated at all times by a natural and frequently impassable barrier from the main province. As the river Potomac is nowhere in express terms reserved by the charter to either colony, it must be reasonably presumed that the intent of the charter of Maryland was, that the rights of Virginia on the southern shores of the Potomac were to remain as they existed by the laws of nature, the laws of nations, and the common law of England, which extended over all British territory.

By these laws, as established by the early authorities and interpreted by modern English and American courts, the right of Virginia to the enjoyment of a river bounding her territory was originally *incident to her lands, and necessarily resulted from their possession.*

In the earliest English treatise upon "riparian rights," it is declared by Lord Hale: "Fresh rivers, of what kind soever, do, of common right, belong to the owers of the soil adjacent, so that the owners on the one side have a common right to the property of the soil, and consequently the right of fishing *usque filum aquæ*, and the owners of the other side the right of soil and ownership, and fishing unto the *filum aquæ* on the other side." (Hale, *de jure maris;* Hargrave's Law Tracts, vol. I, chap. 1.) The same learned writer declares that, even when the proprietorship of a river is secured by grant to a subject, the grant is subject to certain reservations. "But though," says he, "the subject may thus have the property of a navigable river, part of a port, yet these precautions are to be added: 1st, that the king hath got a right of empire or government over it, in reference to the safety of the kingdom, and to his customs, &c.; 2d, that the people have a public interest, a *jus publicum* of passage and re-passage with their goods by water, and must not be obstructed by nuisances, or impeded by exactions, &c., for the *jus privatum* of the owner or proprietor is charged with and subject to that *jus publicum* which belongs to the king's subjects as the soil of a highway is, which, though in point of propriety it may be a private man's freehold, yet is charged with a public interest of the people, which may not be prejudiced or damnified." (Hale, *de jure maris;* Hargrave's Law Tracts, Vol. I, chap. 1.)

The modern English and American courts agree in declaring the right to the use of water of flowing streams to be an *incident* attached to the soil of the lands adjacent to them. "Flowing water," says Chief Baron Pollock, "as well as light and air, are, in one sense, *publici juris.* They are a boon from Providence to all, and differ only in their mode of enjoyment. Light and air are diffused in all directions, flowing water in some. When property was established, each one had the right to enjoy the light and air, and the water flowing through the portion of the soil adjoining to him; the property in the water itself was not in the proprietor of the land through which it passes, but only the use of it, as it passes along, *for the enjoyment of his property, and incident to it.*" (Wood *vs.* Ward, 3 Exchequer Rep. p. 775.) Parke, Baron, says (in Embrey et al. *vs.* Owen, IV Eng. Law and Equity Rep. p. 476) "each proprietor of the adjacent land has the right of the usufruct of the stream which flows through it. * * The right to have the stream to flow in its natural state, without diminution or alteration, is *an incident* to the property in the land through which it passes." Says Mr. Justice Story, "the natural stream, existing by the bounty of Providence for the benefit of the land through which it passes, is *an incident annexed by the operation of law to the land itself.*" (Tyler et al. *vs.* Wilkinson et al. 4 Mason, p. 401.)

Chancellor Kent says, (Commentaries, Vol. III, p. 411,) "It was a settled principle of the common law, that owners of banks of fresh water rivers, above the ebbing and flowing of the tide, had the exclusive right of fishing, as well as the right of property opposite to their respective lands, *ad filum aquæ.*"

The ablest writers on international law insist upon the right to the common use of rivers flowing through adjoining States. In the case of the Twe Gebroeders, (3 Robinson, p. 349,) Sir William Scott observes, " In rivers flowing through continuous States, a common use to different States is presumed ;" and although he admits that by legal *possibility* there may be a peculiar property excluding the common use, he declares that the general presumption bears strongly against such exclusive rights. Mr. Wheaton (Laws of Nations, p. 508) remarks "that when the right of the United States to participate with Spain in the navigation of the Mississippi previous to the cession of Louisiana, was asserted by the American Government on the sentiment, written in deep characters on the heart of man, that the ocean is free to all men, and its rivers to all riparian inhabitants," such being the rights which attached to the shores of Virginia upon the Potomac, by nature, the laws of nations, the laws of England as they existed at the time of the charter of Maryland, the sundering of their rights in manifest opposition to public convenience cannot be derived from the general terms of the sovereign charter. As the Supreme Court says in the case of Hendly Lessee *vs.* Anthony et al., (3 Wharton, p. 374, " in great questions which concern the boundaries of States, where great natural boundaries are established in general terms with a view to public convenience and the avoidance of controversy, the great object, where it can be distinctly perceived, ought not to be defeated by those technical perplexities which may sometimes influence contracts between individuals." The intent to deprive the lands of Virginia of their riparian rights is nowhere precisely expressed in the charter of Maryland, nor is it to be inferred from its general tenor. The English law holds that "a king's grant shall not enure to any other extent than that which is precisely expressed in the grant." (2d Blackstone's Commentaries, p. 347.) "The wise policy of the English law," says Sir William Scott, "interprets grants of the Crown by other rules than those which are applied in the construction of grants of individuals. Against an individual it is presumed that he meant to convey a benefit with the utmost liberality that his words will bear. It is indifferent to the public in which person an interest remains, whether in the granter or taker. With regard to the grant of sovereign, it is far otherwise. It is not held by the sovereign himself as private property, and no alienation shall be presumed except that which is clearly and indisputably expressed." (5 Rob. Adm. Rep. 182.)

The enjoyment of the Potomac river was a public necessity to Virginia. This river was the natural highway which Providence has established for an extent of three hundred miles of her territory. The river was inseparably connected with the adjoining lands, and its use for passage of persons and goods, for fishing and fowling, for sustenance to men and cattle, for irrigation, for mill sites, for grinding corn, for preparing materials for habitations, was indispensable to the full enjoyment of her lands. The use of the river was *id sine quo res uti non potuit.* If the charter of Maryland had, even in express terms, given the river to the new province, the privileges in the river which attached by necessity to the Virginia lands would be held in law to have been reserved. Thus it held that if a man hath several distinct parcels of enclosed lands, and sells all but one surrounded by others, and to which he has no way of passage except over one of the lots he has sold, he has a right of way against his own deed, although he may have been so improvident as to reserve none. The law reserves to him a right of way, in such case, from necessity. It holds that there is an implied restriction incident to the grant, and that it cannot be supposed the granter meant to deprive himself of all use of his remaining land. (3 Kent's Commentaries, pp. 422, 424.) By parity of reasoning, it is to be presumed that the Crown, whether still retaining the proprietorship of the lands of Virginia or as guardian of a colony which was a portion of its realm, could not have intended to deprive itself or the people of the use of the Virginia shores.

It would be difficult to imagine a grant more contrary to reason and nature, or more prejudicial to the interests of the Commonwealth, than one whose effect would be to exclude a vast territory from the use and enjoyment of a great river washing its shores. Such a grant, the law of England renders void from its unreasonableness, as it presumes that the king could not have intended an unwise or unreasonable act. As Blackstone says, (2 Commentaries 246,) "The king, moreover, is not only incapable of *doing*, but even of thinking wrong; he can never mean to do an improper thing; in him is no folly or weakness, and therefore if the crown should be induced to grant any franchise or privilege to a subject contrary to reason or in anywise prejudicial to the Commonwealth or a private person, the law will not suppose the king to have meant either an unwise or injurious action, but declares that the king was deceived in his grant, and thereupon such grant is rendered void."

The preceding authorities and considerations lead to the following conclusions:

1. The primary object of the charter of 1632 in fixing the southern boundary of Maryland, was, to carefully separate the new province from Virginia, which therefore would have been defeated if the legal effect of the charter had been to give Maryland the right of encroachment on the Virginia shore.

2. The right to use the water of the Potomac was, by nature, the laws of nations, and the common law, incident to the Virginia bank or shores.

3. No intent of the king in the charter of Maryland to sunder from the soil the riparian rights which attached to her shore by nature and law, is to be presumed, because no such intent is clearly and indisputably expressed.

4. The free use of the water of the Potomac was a necessity for the enjoyment of the Virginia lands, still remaining in the sovereign granter, and the law implies a reservation in the grant to Maryland of the privileges necessary for the approach to and enjoyment of the Virginia shores.

5. The alienation by royal grant of the natural rights which attached to the Virginia soil, would have been contrary to reason and prejudicial to public good; if the grant of 1632 had such an effect, it would to that extent be rendered void.

6. Hence it follows, that notwithstanding the charter of 1632, the owners of the Toulson tract on the Potomac river have full riparian rights to the centre of the river.

II. Assuming that the charter of Maryland was not subject to the restriction of full riparian rights in the Potomac as above contended, the rights of Maryland under that charter extend only to low water mark on the Virginia shore.

A plain construction of that charter leads to the conclusion, that its intent was to make the *river* the boundary between the two States. We have already adverted to the political reasons which led to the selection of a natural boundary which should carefully separate naturally conflicting jurisdictions. It is most reasonable to presume that the charter intended the river as the boundary. "In case of doubt," says Vattel, "every country lying upon a river is presumed to have no other limits than the river itself; because nothing is more natural than to take a river for a boundary when a State is established on its borders, and wherever there is a doubt, that is always to be presumed which is most natural and most probable." (Laws of Nations, Lib. 1, chap. 22 §268.)

Historians and jurists concur in regarding the river Potomac, not the Virginia bank, as the boundary of Maryland. Bancroft, writing of Maryland, says, "The ocean, the fortieth parallel of latitude, the meridian of the western fountain of the Potomac, *the river itself from its source to its mouth*, &c., these were the limits of the territory." (History Vol. 1 p.242.) Chancellor Bland, who in his decisions has exhibited no little anxiety to extend the jurisdiction of Maryland on its southern borders, speaks of the claim of the plaintiff in Binney's case, as " one which has been deduced from the upper portion of a great and valuable river, belonging altogether to this State, and forming its southern boundary." (Bland's Chancery Reports, Vol. III, p. 123.)

The language of the charter itself, although it does not in express terms declare the *river* to be the boundary, can have no other reasonable intent. The charter gives to Maryland certain territories on the south, *within* certain limits. It extends a line from the head-waters of the river, " *ad ulteriorem ripam dicti fluminis.*" The line extends only " *ad ulteriorem ripam,*" and Maryland lies within the line. It is important to examine the peculiar force which exists, carefully considered, in the Latin words of the charter—a force which is lost in the English version. The line itself is made to extend " AD *ripam.*" The use of this word " AD" distinctly excludes the idea of any encroachment upon the bank, or of extending the limits of Maryland beyond that impassable line which separates the river from the bank. There is a precision of meaning in the word " AD" which is not expressed in the English word *to.* Leverett's dictionary defines the word as follows: " AD, (shortened from *apud* ; others differently,) preposition governing the accusative, signifying motion to a place: *in quo differt ab* IN, *quæ notat ingressum loci,* AD *vero vicinitatem,* e. g. *venire ad urbem, est Romam accedere, venire in urbem, Romam ingredi,*" (which differs from *in*, which expresses the entrance into a place, but *ad* expresses nearness to a place ; thus to come *to* the city is to approach Rome—to come *into* the city, to enter Rome.) That this is no new nor hypercritical view of the force of the expression "*ad ripam,*" is shown by the views taken in an analogous case, where important questions of international rights were in discussion. Says Mr. Wheaton, in his Elements of International Law, "In a controversy between the kingdom of the Netherlands and other States interested in the commerce of the Rhine, the Dutch government claimed the exclusive right of regulating and imposing duties upon the trade and navigation within its own territories, at the places where the different branches into which the Rhine divides itself fall into the sea. The expression in the treaties, '*jusque a la mer*'—*to the sea*—was said to be different in its import from the term *into the sea.*"

From the precise meaning of the words of the charter, the line of Maryland did not rest upon or even touch the further bank. If we could imagine that line to be materially embodied, it would rest wholly on the plane of the river, approaching indefinitely the Virginia bank; Maryland, extending only to the verge of the plane, and debarred by the exclusive meaning of the words "*ad ripam*" from encroaching upon the land, had the further edge of the water, and consequently the river for her boundary, as completely as if it had been declared in express terms.

In Handly's Lessee *vs.* Anthony, (5 Wheaton's Rep. 374,) it was held by the Supreme Court of the United States that when a river is the boundary, the line of boundary is at low water mark; and this rule was adopted upon considerations of public convenience, which are peculiarly applicable to this case. In the case referred to, ejectment was brought in the Circuit Court of the District of Kentucky to recover land which the plaintiff claimed under a grant from the State of Virginia, and which the defendant held under a grant from the United States as being part of Indiana. The title depended upon the question whether the lands lay in the State of Kentucky or the State of Indiana. Chief Justice Marshall, in delivering the opinion of the Court, says: "In January, 1781, the Commonwealth of Virginia yielded to the United States all title and claim which the said Commonwealth had to the territory northwest of the Ohio, subject to the conditions annexed to said act of cession. One of those conditions is, 'that the ceded territory shall be laid out and formed into States.'

"It was intended, then, by Virginia, when she made this cession to the United States, and most probably when she opened her land office, that the great river Ohio should constitute a boundary between the States which might be formed on its opposite banks. This intention ought never to be disregarded in construing this cession. * *

"The questions presented are whether land is properly denominated an island of the Ohio, unless it be surrounded with the water of the river when low; and whether Kentucky was bounded on the west and northwest by the low water mark of the river or its middle state; or in other words, whether the State of Indiana extends to low water mark, or stops at the line reached by the river when at its medium height?

"In pursuing this inquiry we must recollect that it is not the bank of the river, but the river itself, at which the cession of Virginia commences. She conveys to Congress all her right to the territory "situate, lying and being to the northwest of the river Ohio," and this territory, according to express stipulation, is to be laid off into independent States. These States, then, are to have the river itself, whatever that may be, for its boundary. This is a natural boundary, and in establishing it, Virginia must have had in view the convenience of the future population of the country.

"When a great river is the boundary between two nations or States, if the original property is in neither, and there be no convention respecting it, each holds to the middle of the stream; but when, as in this case, one State is the original proprietor, and grants the territory on one side only, it retains the river within its own domain, and the newly created State extends to the river only. The river, however, is the boundary."

Again, through the Chief Justice, the Court say: "If instead of an annual and somewhat irregular rising and falling of the river, it was a daily and almost regular ebbing and flowing of the tide, it would not be doubted that a country bounded by a river would extend to low water mark. This rule has been established by the common consent of mankind; it is founded upon common convenience. Even when a State retains its domain over a river which constitutes the boundary between itself and another State, it would be extremely inconvenient to extend its dominion over the land on the other side which was left bare by the receding of the water. And this inconvenience is not less where the rising and falling is annual, than where it is diurnal. Whenever the river is the boundary between States, it is the main, the permanent river, which constitutes the boundary; and the mind will find itself embarrassed with insuperable difficulty in attempting to draw any other line than the low water mark."

These views would seem to establish, beyond all question, the title of Virginia to low water mark on the Potomac. But it is contended by Judge Brewer that the expressions of the charter of Maryland, fixing its southern line, are substantially the same as those used by the State of Georgia in its grant referred to in Howard *vs.* Ingersoll, (13 Howard, p. 381,) in which case the Supreme Court held that the dividing line on the Chatahoochee river, between the States of Georgia and Alabama, was on the top of the high western bank of the river, leaving the bed of the river and the western shelving shore within the State of Georgia. We cannot concur in the opinion that the line fixed by the two grants is substantially the same, or that the "beginning of the dividing line in both grants is on the bank, and so far they are identical."

The expressions in the grant of Georgia are, "west of a line beginning *on* the western bank of the Chatahoochee river where the same crosses the boundary line between the United States and Spain, running thence up the Chatahoochee and along the bank." The line was required to run both *on* and *along* the bank. The Court being thus excluded from adopting the line of low water mark fixed in the case of Handly Lessee, &c.,

which Mr. Justice Wilson admits he should greatly have preferred if the terms of the cession had justified such an interpretation, were compelled to adopt some natural line *upon* the bank which could be at all times easily traced. They therefore adopted that line where the action of the water has permanently marked itself on the soil.

The object sought for by the Court is well explained by Mr. Justice Curtis, who says: "The act of cession is silent as to the particular part of the bank *on* which the line is to be run. But, inasmuch as it must be run *on* some part of the bank, we are obliged to resort to the presumed intentions of the commissioners and the parties, inferable from the nature of the line as a line of boundary of political jurisdiction as well as of proprietorship; and according to that presumed intention we must declare it to be on that part of the bank which will best promote the convenience and advantage of both parties, and most fully accomplished the apparent and leading purpose to establish a natural boundary." The conflicting opinions of the Court as to the reasoning of the decision show the great difficulty they had in fixing this natural boundary upon the bank. This case has no authority, either in its decision or the reasoning of the Court, xcept in cases where a line is to be seen *on* and *along* the bank. We have shown that the line of Maryland was excluded by the precise words of the charter from running *on* the bank. No such indefinite or uncertain line as the Court was compelled to establish in the case last referred to is required. The line adopted by the Court in Handly Lessee, as one established by the common consent of mankind, and founded upon common convenience, may be adopted with strict conformity to the charter which fixed the boundary.

III. The territory of Virginia extends, *by prescription*, to low water mark on the Potomac, and includes wharves, dams, and other improved property extending from the Virginia shore to the middle thread of the stream, which do not injure or obstruct the navigation.

The rights accruing to one State against another by prescription are clearly established. Says Mr. Wheaton, in his treatise on the Elements of International Law, p. 218, "The writers on natural law have questioned how far that peculiar species of presumption arising from the lapse of time, which is called prescription, is justly applicable as between nation and nation. But the constant and approved practice of nations shows that by whatever name it may be called, the uninterrupted possession of territory or other species of property for a certain length of time by one State excludes the claim of every other, in the same manner as by the laws of nature, and the municipal code of every civilized nation, a similar possession by an individual excludes the claim of every other person to the article of property in question. This rule is founded upon the supposition, confirmed by constant experience, that every person will naturally seek to enjoy that which belongs to him, and the inference fairly to be drawn from his silence and neglect of the original defect of his title, or his intention to relinquish it." In the case of Rhode Island *vs.* Massachusetts, (IV Howard, page 639,) the Supreme Court say, "For the security of rights, whether of persons or individuals, long possession under a claim of title is protected, and there is no controversy in which this great principle may be involved with greater justice and propriety than in a case of disputed boundary." In the case of Handly Lessee *vs.* Anthony, before quoted, where there was a question of boundary between Kentucky and Indiana, the same Court say, "it is a fact of no inconsiderable importance in this case, that the inhabitants of this land have uniformly considered themselves as belonging to the last mentioned State."

Ancient jurisdiction is not determined by the mere assertion of right, but by formal acts of possession. The character of the acts which must be proved to establish possession, is clearly laid down by the most eminent English authority on international laws. Says Sir William Scott, (3 Robinson, 346,) "Ancient jurisdiction is proved by formal acts of authority; by holding courts of conservancy of the navigation; by ceremonious processions to ascertain the boundaries, in the nature of perambulations; by marked distinctions in maps and charts prepared under public inspection and control; by laying of tolls; by exclusive fisheries; by permanent and visible emblems of power there established; by the appointment of officers specially designated to that station; by stationary guardships; by records and muniments showing that the right has always been asserted, and whenever resisted, resisted with effect. This is the natural evidence to be looked for generally; and such as it is more particularly reasonable to require where a right is claimed against all general principles, and against the natural rights and limits, and indeed against the independence and security of neighboring States."

The character of the claim set up for Maryland on the Virginia shore could not be more aptly described than in the preceding paragraph. What single act of occupancy has the State of Maryland ever exercised on the Southern shores of the Potomac, or when has her Legislature ever asserted a right to such occupancy? The bed of the river, from the middle thread to the top of the further bank, including the shelving shores, and thus necessarily including valuable meadows, all the mill sites, the exclusive rights of fishing and fowling, of collecting drift wood, of supplying water for domestic use and irrigation, and of establishing ferries and bridges, all this is claimed to belong to Maryland, and yet Judge Brewer admits that this invaluable tract has never been granted by the State, and therefore the first act of assertion of right and occupancy has yet to be performed.

On the other hand, Virginia, in her Constitution in 1776 and her revised code in 1849, claimed the title, under the charter of James of 1609, " to the free navigation of the rivers Potomac and Pocomoke, with the property of the Virginia shores and strands bordering on either of said rivers, and all the improvements thereon," without reference to tide water, and continued to assert and exercise this right by various legislative acts. Some of these may be briefly enumerated. In 1748, ferries were established by the law of Virginia from five different points on the Potomac, to the Maryland shore. In 1786 a ferry was established by the Legislature, from land in the county of Loudoun across the Potomac river to land on the opposite shore in the State of Maryland. In 1794, authority was given by the State of Virginia to the United States to purchase Harper's Ferry for an arsenal. In 1796, and 1797, a purchase was made of three or four hundred acres of land, and an island on the Potomac, containing twenty acres, on which the dam abuts, all being described as being in the county of Berkeley, Virginia, where the deeds were recorded. Virginia emphatically asserted the riparian rights of her citizens on the Potomac by the act in relation to the Potomac Company, (passed October, 1784,) which is as follows:

Sec. 12, and preamble to sec. 13. And whereas some of the places, through which it may be necessary to conduct said canal, may be convenient for erecting mills, forges, and other water works, and the persons, possessors of such situations, may design to improve the same, and it is the intention of this act not to interfere with private property, but for the purpose of improving and perfecting the said navigation:

"13. Be it enacted, That the water, or any part thereof, conveyed through any canal or cut made by the said company, shall not be used for any purpose but navigation, unless the consent of the proprietors of the land through which the same shall be led be first had; and the said president and directors, or a majority of them, are hereby empowered and directed, if it can be conveniently done to answer both the purposes of navigation and water works aforesaid, to enter into reasonable agreement with the proprietors of such situation, concerning the just proportion of the expenses of making large canals or cuts capable of carrying such quantities of water as may be sufficient for the purposes of navigation, and also for any such water works as aforesaid." (Davis' Laws of District of Columbia, appendix, p. 452.)

The rights of Virginia in the Potomac were asserted by the act of the General Assembly of that State, passed January 7th, 1800, providing for the prevention of obstructions to the navigation of the river above tide water.

The riparian rights of the owners of the "Toulson tract" were asserted by the act of 1852 incorporating "The Great Falls Manufacturing Company," for the purpose of manufacturing cotton, etc., and for improving the water power at or near the Great Falls of the Potomac river, in the county of Fairfax, and also by the act to incorporate "The Farmers' Milling Company," for the purpose of manufacturing flour and other things, at the Great Falls of the Potomac, in the county of Fairfax.

It cannot be denied that the owners of the shores, mill sites and other improvements on the southern border of the Potomac, have uniformly considered them as belonging to Virginia, a fact which the Supreme Court has declared to be "of no inconsiderable importance in ascertaining the boundaries of a State."

We are of the opinion that Virginia has exercised jurisdiction, without opposition from Maryland, over the southern shores of the Potomac, and the improvements thereon, under a claim of title, for a sufficient length of time to establish a prescriptive right to them as within her territory; and that although the owners of the Toulson tract on the Potomac could not, on the principle of *nullum tempus occurit regi*, set up as individuals their prescriptive rights against Maryland, they have, by their grant from Virginia, a title to all lands and improvements on the Potomac river within their limits which lie in the territory of Virginia, and have therefore full riparian rights in the Potomac river.

IV. Full riparian rights are secured to the owners of the Toulson tract by the COMPACT between Maryland and Virginia, made in the year 1785, which provides "that the citizens of each State respectively shall have full property in the shores of the Potomac river adjoining their lands, with all emoluments and advantages thereunto belonging, and the privilege of carrying out wharves and other improvements, so as not to obstruct or injure the navigation of the river."

This compact was a treaty between two sovereign States, each having solemnly pledged its faith and honor that the treaty should be forever faithfully and inviolably observed, according to its true intent and meaning. The compact, then, is to be interpreted by those principles of international law which interpret a convention between States, according to the presumed intention of both the high contracting parties, which admit in neither any implied reservation of advantage or privilege, and which presumed in each an exalted honor consistent with its sovereign dignity.

The first general maxim, says Vattel, in the interpretation of treaties is "*that it is not allowed to interpret what has no need of interpretation.* When a deed is worded in clear and precise terms—when its meaning is evident, and leads to no absurd conclusion—there can be no reason for refusing to admit the meaning which such deed naturally presents. To go elsewhere in search of conjectures in order to restrict or extend it, is but an attempt to elude it."

The seventh article of the compact declares that "the citizens of each State respectively shall have full property in the shores of the Potomac river adjoining their lands, with all emoluments and advantages thereunto belonging, and the privilege of making and carrying out wharves and other improvements so as not to injure the navigation of the river." The rights attach to the Potomac river; not to a part of the river, but the river, *the whole river*, from its source to the Bay, wherever it is known as the Potomac river. The words are clear and precise; they can have no other meaning. It is a meaning which leads "to no absurd conclusion," but is the meaning which "the deed naturally presents." To argue from other provisions of the compact, which sufficiently explain themselves without such a construction, that the words "the

Potomac river" mean only that lesser portion of the river extending from the head of tide water to the bay, and that the greater portion, extending from its source to tide water, for a distance of over two hundred miles, constituting almost the only part which can be called the river according to strict geographical definition, is excluded from the operation of the compact, is but an attempt to elude "the clear and precise terms of the convention."

It is clear that *Virginia*, when she became a party to the compact, intended no such restriction. In her constitution, adopted in 1776, the rights which she claimed on her whole northern boundary are clearly defined. The 21st section 2d chapter of the Constitution of Virginia declares as follows: "The territories contained within the charters erecting the colonies of Maryland, etc., are hereby ceded, released and forever confirmed to the people of those colonies respectively, with all rights of property, jurisdiction and government, and all other rights whatsoever, which might, at any time heretofore, have been claimed by Virginia, *except the free navigation and use of the rivers Potomac and Pocomoke, with the property of the Virginia shores, or strands bordering on either of said rivers, and all improvements which have been or shall be made thereon.* The western and northern extent of Virginia, shall, in all other respects, stand as fixed by the charter of James the first, in the year one thousand six hundred and nine."

The Potomac river is spoken of in direct connexion with the whole northern extent of Virginia, and, as forming its northern boundary. It cannot admit of a doubt that the whole river from its source to its mouth was intended. There is not an intimation restricting the application of the provision for the use of the Potomac to the portion from the head of tide water, except that which is pretended to be found in the use of the words "shores or strands," the former of which terms, although sometimes applied to the borders of bays, lakes, and seas, is more strictly applied to the land bordering all bodies of water, between high and low water mark. Virginia, then, by her constitution, claimed the use of the whole of the Potomac river, and for her citizens, the property of the whole shore bordering on the Potomac, and all improvements which have been or shall be made thereon. This property she claimed as within her jurisdiction, and as part of the territory secured to her by the royal charter of 1609. Is there anything in the compact which can be tortured into a relinquishment of this claim, or a cession to Maryland of this portion of her territory? Is it to be conceived that Virginia, when she became a party to a compact which secured, in express terms, all the rights to the Potomac which she claimed under her constitution, could have intended a restriction which would deprive her borders, reaching from the sources of the Potomac to tide water, a territory over two hundred miles in extent, of the uses of the great river which had been so solemnly guaranteed by her constitution?

The compact was concluded only nine years after the adoption of the Virginia constitution. The provisions in the compact respecting the rights in the Potomac, although not absolutely identical in language with those in the constitution, are so similar as to lead to the conlusion that both were intended to accomplish the same object.

The compact of 1785 cannot be rightly interpreted without regarding the spirit of the age and people which induced its execution. Maryland and Virginia, in their common struggles for independence, had forgotten their ancient rivalries. They sought to frame a convention which should settle all former and possible questions of controversy. Their commissioners, in this spirit, sitting at Mount Vernon, provided not only for the common use of the Potomac "for the purpose of navigation and commerce to the citizens of Virginia and Maryland," but for the citizens of "the United States, and all other persons in amity with the said States trading to or from Virginia or Maryland."

We are historically informed that the vexations on other streams of the Old World, were prominent considerations with the statesmen of that period, to lead them to secure the navigable highways of the United States from abuses like those which had afflicted and disgraced the waters of Europe. The compact of 1785, with its provisions of unprecedented liberality, was the immediate precursor of the famous ordinance of the Congress of the Confederation, dated July 13th, 1787, justly styled the Magna Charta of our internal navigation, which declared to the whole American world that "the navigable waters of the Mississippi and St. Lawrence, and the carrying places between the same, shall be common property, and forever free, as well to the inhabitants of the said country, as to the citizens of the United States, and those of any other States that may be admitted into the Confederacy, without any tax, duty, or impost therefor."

It would be a reproach to Maryland to say that she did not fully partake of the magnanimous sentiments which produced these two great compacts, or to suppose that in her compact with Virginia, receiving all that the latter could offer, she could have intended to reserve rights and privileges on the Potomac, above tide water, utterly useless to herself, though vitally important to the sister State with whom she was in solemn covenant.

There can be no doubt about the construction of Virginia as to her rights on the Potomac, and in a compact conceived in the spirit of those times, it must be presumed that wherever Virginia intended, Maryland intended.

The opinion of Chancellor Bland in Binney's case, approved by Judge Brewer, that "there is nothing in this compact which relates in any manner to the river Potomac above tide," seems to be founded simply upon the general purpose of the compact, as shown in its principal provisions, and its title, which recites its object to be "to settle the jurisdiction and navigation of the Potomac river." Although the leading purpose and title of an act may furnish important means for determining the intent of a law, they cannot control distinct and express provisions in the body of the act. It is clear that the compact, in more than one of its articles, referred to subjects unconnected with the jurisdiction and navigation of the Potomac, and had in view portions of the river above tide water, which were not navigable in the ordinary sense of the term. Thus the 12th section provided "that the citizens of either State having lands in the other shall have full liberty to transport to their own State the produce of such lands, or to remove their effects free of duty, tax, or charge whatever, for the liberty to remove such produce or effects." Can it be pretended that the title and leading purpose of the compact limits this right of transport to the waters of the Potomac, or that it does not give the liberty of transporting goods from one State to the other, across all portions of the Potomac, whether above or below tide? Yet this unreasonable, if not absurd, construction must be adopted, if the views derived by the eminent Judges referred to from the general purpose and title of the compact, are correct.

But it is said by Judge Brewer, "Suppose, however, the compact was intended to apply to the river above tide, and that it is to be considered an unnavigable river to which full riparian rights could attach, how were they acquired by the owners of the 'Toulson tract?' Not by the original grant, for that extended only to the bank of the river; not by the cession of the shore by the compact, unless you consider that as extending the original grant to the river, and by implication also to the middle of the stream."

The answer to this is obvious. The owners of the "Toulson tract" do not pretend to claim riparian rights under a cession or grant from Maryland. They claim under Virginia the territorial rights asserted in her constitution to have been established by the charter of 1609. Under that charter Virginia claimed in her constitution "the property of the Virginia shores or strands bordering on the Potomac, and all improvements which have been or shall be made thereon." This claim of Virginia to its full extent was admitted by Maryland when she became a party to the compact which declared that "the citizens of each State respectively shall have full property in the shores of the Potomac adjoining their lands, with all emoluments and advantages thereunto belonging." There is no necessity for considering the compact as a "cession" to Virginia of the shore, or "as extending the original grant to the river" since the rights of Virginia on the Potomac had already been established by a royal charter. The compact was not the foundation of the right, but the solemn recognition of one already existing.

Having shown, as we believe, that the owners of the "Toulson tract" have riparian rights on the Potomac river—1st. Because such rights were originally incident to the Virginia shores, and the rights of Maryland under her charter were subject to them; 2d. By the precise terms of the charter of Maryland; 3d. By prescription; 4th. By the compact admitting the right of Virginia to her shores on the Potomac, and to all emoluments and advantages attached to them—the only remaining question is, what privileges the possession of riparian rights gives to the owners of the "Toulson tract." We cannot answer this question more satisfactorily to ourselves than by quoting from the opinion of John Carroll Brent, Esq., as to the rights and duties of riparian proprietors in their relations with others below them on the same stream, whose views we fully adopt.

"The old common law has it, '*Aqua currit et debet currere ut currere solebat.*' In Williams *vs.* Moreland, 2 B. & Cress. R., 510, it is laid down, 'By all the modern as well as by all the ancient authorities, the right of property in the water is *usufructuary*, and consists not so much of the fluid itself as of the advantage of its *momentum* or *impetus;*' and in Mayor, &c. *vs.* Commissioners of Spring Garden, (Penn. 7 Barr R., 348,) 'And the grant by a legislature of a State of the water power of a navigable stream, does not pass to the grantee the title to the *corpus* of the water, or prevent its use by others. *The owner of the land merely transmits the water over the surface; he receives as much from his higher neighbor as he sends down to his neighbor below;* he is *neither better nor worse; the level of the water remains the same.*' (Per Tindal,

C. J., in Acton *vs.* Blundell, 12 M. and Welsb. R., 324.) This right to apply the water of a water-course is so forcibly and distinctly described and limited in the language of Angell, and his extracts from the opinions of some of our most illustrious judges, that I feel myself authorized to apply them, in their full force and effect, to those of the proprietors at the Falls. At section 95, Angell says: 'In a case in this country of much more than ordinary importance, and one universally and frequently appealed to as of high authority, the general doctrine in relation to the right to the water of a water-course is thus laid down by Mr. Justice Story: 2. "*Prima facie*, every proprietor on each bank of a river is entitled to the land covered with water to the middle thread of the stream, or, as commonly expressed, *usque ad filum aquæ*." (2. In Tyler *vs.* Wilkinson, 4 Mason's Cir. Co. R., 400.) In virtue of this ownership, he has a right to the use of the water flowing over it, in its natural current, *without diminution or obstruction*. But, strictly speaking, he has no property in the water itself, but a simple use of it while it passes along. *The consequence of this principle is, that no proprietor has a right to use the water to the prejudice of another.*' 'This,' adds the same high authority, 'is the necessary result of the perfect equality of right among all the proprietors of that which is common to all.'

"The general right of the riparian proprietors to the use of the water has been defined with ability and clearness by another of our learned judges. 'The water power,' says he, 'to which the riparian owner is entitled, consists in the fall in the stream, when in its natural state, as it passes through his land, or along the boundary of it; or, in other words, it consists of the difference between the surface where the stream first touches his land, and the surface where it leaves it.' (Per Ch. Justice Gibson, of Pa., in M'Calmont *vs.* Whitaker, 3 Rawles' Penn. R., 84.) No single proprietor can alter the level of the water where it *enters* or where it *leaves* his property. In the language of the Vice-Chancellor, in Wright *vs.* Howard, 1 Sim.

& Stu. Ch. R., 203, 'Without the consent of the other proprietors, who may be affected by his operations, no proprietor can either diminish the quantity of water which would descend to the proprietor below, nor throw the water back upon the proprietors above. Every proprietor who claims either to throw the water back, or diminishes the quantity which is to descend below, must, in order to maintain his claim, *either prove an actual grant or license fron the proprietors affected by his operations*, or must prove an uninterrupted enjoyment of twenty yeasr. If a person stop the current of a stream, which has immediately flowed in a different direction, and thereby prejudices rnother, he subjects himself to an action.' (Saunders *vs.* Neuman, 1 B. & Ald. R., 258.) So 'any impediment,' says the Supreme Court of Pennsylvania, 'in the stream caused by the defendant's dam, by which the plaintiff's mill is stopped from grinding, in any state of the water, or made to grind slower or worse than it otherwise would, is an injury for which the plaintiff would be entitled to damages.'" (Butz *vs.* Ihrie, 2 Rawles' Penn. R., 218.)

In view of these authorities, we are clearly of the opinion that the riparian rights attached to the "Toulson tract" cannot be destroyed, abridged or diminished by any person or authority, whether by permanent diversion of the water from its natural flow at or near said tract, or from any upper portion of the stream, without right of remedy by action at law, or restraint and injunction by a Court of Equity.

Respectfully, your obedient servants,

REVERDY JOHNSON,
JOHN L. HAYES.

www.ingramcontent.com/pod-product-compliance
Lightning Source LLC
LaVergne TN
LVHW011142110826
845150LV00008B/2467
9781418192839